Olivia Montuschi

Olivia Montuschi is the mother of two donor conceived adults, born in 1983 and 1986. She and her husband Walter Merricks founded the Donor Conception Network with four other families in 1993. Olivia trained as a teacher and a counsellor and for many years worked as a parenting educator and trainer, writing materials and running parenting education programmes. She now works part-time as Practice Consultant to DC Network.

Contents

Acknowledgements and thanks

This revised edition of Telling and Talking 12 – 16 is for parents who are planning to 'tell' or to add information about a second donor for the first time. It takes some of the information from the original booklet, but also has updated references to influences in young people's lives and a considerable amount of new material.   For the latter I am indebted to Jane Ellis, my colleague at the Donor Conception Network who has a great deal of experience of talking with donor conceived young people who are finding out for the first time about their beginnings.

Enormous thanks go to Marilyn Crawshaw and Ken Daniels who contributed significantly to the original booklet and continue to inspire everything I write and to Elizabeth Howell for her depth of knowledge and experience of working with parents and children.

I could not have embarked on the writing of this booklet without the support, encouragement and eagle eyes on each draft, of my colleagues Nina, Jo, Yael and Lucia in the DC Network office.

Olivia Montuschi
March 2019

Telling and Talking
12 – 16

"As we have progressed together through this maze and learned to trust each other, the flood of communication has been amazing."

This booklet is for parents who have built or added to their families with the help of sperm, egg, double or embryo donation (with or without the use of surrogacy) and have children between the ages of 12 and 16 who do not yet know that they are donor conceived. Or your child might know about only one of their donors in the case of double or embryo donation or about the surrogate but not the egg donor where surrogacy has been used.

Over the next few pages you will find
- acknowledgement that you may have some very mixed feelings about telling and talking about this subject,
- practical suggestions about how you can prepare yourself for such conversations
- insight into the potential feelings and responses of your child or children
- guidance on setting the scene for telling for the first time, language to use on this occasion and ways to follow-up afterwards
- information about what is happening developmentally for your children at this stage of their lives
- tips on how they may react or respond to donor conception issues at home and at school.

Throughout the booklet you will find quotes from donor conceived young people and their parents, and finally the comments of two mothers.

Although infertility is the reason why most heterosexual couples have used donor conception, some of you will have done so in order to avoid passing on a genetic condition. Single people, lesbians and gay couples are all in need of gametes from the opposite sex. Some people also need to use a surrogate. The principles involved in telling and the vast majority of this booklet are relevant for all family types.

Deciding to Tell

Coming to this decision may or may not have been difficult, although it would be unusual if you didn't have some mixed feelings about the actual occasion of 'telling'.

You may have always planned to tell at this age, believing that your child would be old enough to understand by this time. Or it could be that you had planned to tell earlier but the right time didn't seem to occur and the years just slipped by. Alternatively you or your partner might have originally decided to keep the secret, but minds have changed since then.

If you are a male couple who have used surrogacy and a separate egg donor, it may not be until your child comes across information about genetics and biological heritage at school and starts to ask questions, that you realise that information about your egg donor has been absent in your child's life. This may also be true for other parent(s) who have used double or embryo donation to create their family but have so far only told their child about the sperm donor.

Secrecy and Anonymity

Although the climate of secrecy that prevailed in UK clinics was largely over by the early 2000's, many clinics remained sceptical for some time about the relevance or necessity of telling children about being donor conceived. They moved much further towards acceptance of openness with the child and others with the removal of anonymity for donors in 2005. The Human Fertilisation and Embryology Authority (HFEA) now requires all UK clinics to encourage and prepare people undergoing donor conception treatment to tell their children about their origins from an early age and inform potential parents where they can find materials to help with this.

Although anonymity for donors has now ended in the UK and in a few countries in Northern Europe, many British citizens use clinics abroad (some promoted by UK clinics) where donors remain anonymous and sharing information with children is not always encouraged. Surrogacy arrangements abroad are also very different to the UK so many male couples in particular may be unaware of how the culture of donation in the UK has changed over the years.

You will have conceived your child or children either in the UK or abroad, during a time when ideas about 'telling' children were in transition from secrecy to openness. Your choice of clinic may or may not have reflected your views on 'telling'. We now know from many donor conceived adults and teenagers that they believe every donor conceived child should be given as much information as possible about their biological origins, ideally from an early age. One donor conceived adult known to DC Network has said that 'openness' as a state of mind within families is preferable to using the term 'telling' as the latter could refer to a one-off act, whilst the former infers a process that continues over a lifetime.

Preparing to Tell

Thinking about 'telling' your child may bring up strong feelings for you. It may make you feel sick with fear about rejection. You might be anxious about causing a rift in the family or damage to your child. These feelings, some focused on you and some on your child, are very normal. When preparing to share information with your child it can be helpful to think about what you need to do to be ready yourself (the focus being on you) and what you need to take into account with regard to your child (the focus being on them). Asking yourself questions in these two different ways can help prevent your head swirling with unfocused anxiety and fear. Good starting points are –

- What 'telling' means for you: how you and your partner, if you have one, are feeling now about the infertility of one or both of you (or other condition

or situation that led you to use donor conception) and your decision to use egg, sperm, double or embryo donation.
- The stage of development of your child and what is happening in their life at the moment

Parents, 'telling' and the past

It is likely that something has triggered the need to share information with your child now. It may be that you feel you have no choice about 'telling' because there is a strong chance that your child will learn from another source first. Possibly your teenager or another family member has seen TV advertisements for direct-to-consumer DNA tests and suggested it would be fun for you all to be tested. Some parents find themselves in a situation where they have developed a serious medical condition with heritable components and medical staff are suggesting that their children are tested for this condition.

Whatever your situation, you may well find that despite wanting to concentrate on the here and now of 'telling' you are full of thoughts and feelings from the time of your fertility treatment and deciding on donor conception. Although, as I described earlier, the culture was just beginning to change when you had your treatment, you may not have had the opportunity of counselling before treatment and many doctors certainly remained ambivalent about 'telling' at that time. You may have been one of the first people to go abroad for egg donation, perhaps when donors were still anonymous in the UK or just after the ending of anonymity in 2005 when egg donors were scarce in the UK. If that is the case your donor will have been anonymous and you may have very little information about her.

If your feelings about your infertility or the choices you made at the time of treatment are getting in the way of talking with your partner or others or making you feel nervous about sharing the information with your child, it is likely to be helpful to talk with a good friend or a professional like a counsellor before telling your child. DC Network is always happy to help and support you at this time. We can also give you names of counsellors who are knowledgeable about donor conception families.

Donor conceived young people need their parents to be able to handle the range of complex, contradictory and sometimes quite strong feelings that may result from being 'told' no matter how old or mature they seem. If you are pre-occupied with your own thoughts and feelings, you are less likely to be able to 'be there' emotionally for your child and to engage with their reactions without becoming anxious and defensive.

If the prospect of 'telling' fills you with dread, try looking at what makes you want to keep it a secret. The list might include: not wanting your family to be different, fear that your child will reject you as 'not their real parent' in favour of an unknown donor, fear that your child will be forever confused about her identity or you and family will be stigmatised in some way – that in general it will do more harm than good.

Then try making a list of the reasons you believe that being open with your child is the right thing to do: they are likely to include fostering honesty and trust, encouraging your child's healthy identity development, and ensuring secrets do not seriously damage your parent-child relationship, particularly if the news came out unexpectedly.

And consider the positives you have on your side in talking to your older child: you are more likely to be comfortable and secure with the bond between you and your child, and more confident that you are attuned to their character so you know how to support them best, even if teenage behaviour is making life a bit bumpy at the moment. You are aware by now that you are far from being a 'different' sort of family; you are just one amongst many types of family that don't need to be genetically connected to be successful.

Thinking it through and re-visiting your earlier thoughts can help you feel more positive about your decision to tell and aware of your own vulnerabilities.

Loss and fertility

Most of you will have used donor conception to create your family because you were not able to have your own longed for biological child. Grieving infertility and such a loss (and for some single women, grieving the loss of a plan to have a family together with a partner) has now been recognised as part of an important process that needs to start before you have treatment and may continue in different ways over many years. For lesbian and gay couples loss may be more about not being able to have the child of a loved partner or because of having to own your sexuality more publicly than you have previously chosen to do.

For many people infertility is a hidden and private grief that can mean it is hard to acknowledge: it can make it feel that you don't have any right to talk about it. If you were not supported in taking your time to start a grieving process at the time of diagnosis then it can help to revisit some of those feelings now. Although it may not feel comfortable – old memories can trigger regret, anger or distress - allowing some of those emotions to come through can help to clarify how you feel now. The awareness of loss and your whole fertility journey belong to you, as an individual or a couple. Your child, in turn may experience a sense of loss too (of identity, trust in the family, genetic inheritance) either at the time of being told or later as they grow up - or they may feel completely differently. It can be helpful to remember that loss itself does not have to be damaging if it is responded to with understanding and empathy. If you are able to access support for yourself in advance, you will then be in a better position to 'be there' emotionally for your child and avoid the risk of possibly becoming overwhelmed by emotion that belongs to your past experiences.

The two quotes below are from mothers, one genetic, one non-genetic who are reflecting back on their feelings from the beginning of their donor conception journey –

Gill has boy/girl twins, now aged 12, by egg donation, " I struggled through what I now know was a grieving process and had to be honest with myself about my own feelings in order to come to terms with, and embrace, the idea of a child that would not be genetically connected to me. It made me explore the very reasons we want to have children – that wish to carry on, or even to hold on to, family we have lost. I feel that, because of all this soul searching, from very early on I saw my potential child as an individual – very much their own person (or people as it turned out) rather than a mini-me."

Ali's daughter was conceived by sperm donation, "It's hard, in this situation, to acknowledge your own sense of loss because it seems less than your partner's. They are the ones coping with not being able to contribute their genes to their children, while what you have lost (not seeing your loved partner physically in your kids) seems relatively minor in comparison...talking about feeling sadness...can be perceived by your partner as being their 'fault'...for my husband and me, identifying together as an 'infertile couple' has helped."

Non-genetic parents and telling

In some families the parent who is not genetically connected may feel that they have most to lose from their child being told. Not only might they fear rejection and anger, but some parents are apprehensive about exposing their infertility, especially if they have avoided acknowledging it over the years. They may believe that it brings stigma and shame to them or their child. This is a very understandable fear but it is not a reason to take a back seat when it comes to telling. Your children will need you and want you to talk with them. They will take their lead from you and your attitude to donor conception.

Donor conceived Australian older teenager Geraldine Hewitt reports in her research Missing Links, an exploration of identity issues for donor conceived people, that..."Many offspring expressed regret that their parents, especially their social father, had been unable to be honest with them, with one participant stating that, 'I felt incredible regret that my father felt afraid to share this information with me. We could have had a very close relationship if he had not been ashamed of his infertility.' "

Genetic parents and 'telling'

It is not always the non-genetic parent who is most anxious about 'telling'. Sometimes the parent who is genetically connected has complicated feelings associated with fear of their partner being rejected or sometimes shame and stigma around using donor conception for family creation. Or there may be guilt about not having 'told' earlier and fear of a negative reaction from your child. If you are one of these parents you may not even fully understand yourself why the thought of 'telling' feels so difficult.

Sometimes it can be difficult to know how or when to disclose information about your child's donor conception in a way that doesn't break a partner's confidence. Ali, speaking about a session held at a DC Network conference said this. "Some men, like my partner, are incredibly open in theory and yet sometimes still not totally comfortable discussing in the moment...what is tricky is to feel able to share the information when you need to, because so often you feel as though you are revealing something too personal about your partner… we talked about how having a general conversation with your partner about the kinds of situations in which you might disclose, might help you feel more confident in talking with others, knowing you have their blessing."

Doing the 'telling' alone when you started parenting as a couple

In an ideal world both parents would share news with their child about how they came to be part of their family. But there are many reasons why you may be contemplating taking this on alone. Maybe your partner has died and you now feel free to talk about something he or she would have found embarrassing and difficult. You may be divorced, or you and your partner still may not agree about 'telling' but you believe this is something you have to do.

Whatever your situation, one of these scenarios is likely to apply –
- *Either* you are free to make this decision alone, because your partner has died or has long lost contact with you and your child
- *Or* the person you went into parenthood with remains in contact or is easily contactable and therefore needs to be consulted or their views at least taken into account.

If you are free to undertake the telling alone, all the guidance offered here is relevant to you, but it is particularly important to take time to think through your own feelings first and find yourself some back-up. It is possible that you will be on the receiving end of anger and other feelings that are all the stronger because your parenting partner is no longer around and because of your child's stage of development. Your response may be in turn to feel angry or sad yourself. It is helpful if you can acknowledge these feelings to yourself but express them elsewhere. Your child needs your robust support above anything else so it is not appropriate to spill out your own strong feelings in front of your child.

If you are *not* free to undertake the telling alone, again all the guidance here is relevant but this is a much trickier situation. Individual circumstances will vary enormously, but if the young person concerned has a relationship, no matter how remote, with your partner or ex-partner then this person has a right to be consulted or at the very least informed about your wish or intention to tell. If your ex-partner objects to your intention to tell you may be facing acute dilemmas as a result of this dispute. If this is the case and you are still in a legally sanctioned relationship with the person who is named on your child's birth certificate as mother or father, you may want to seek legal advice if you have not already done so. The courts will judge these situations by assessing what is in the best interest of your child – which, subject to appropriate timing, will mean that your child should be told the truth. Even if the courts are not involved, it is possible that your ex-partner may feel so attacked and disempowered by your decision to tell, that s/he may behave in unpredictable ways that are not in the interest of your child.

It will be very important for you to think through very carefully your reasons for wanting to tell now. These may be quite complex, but remember that from your child's point of view the only valid reason is their need and right to have this information about themselves. All reasonable steps should be taken to involve and include the other parent in the preparation process, even if they are unwilling or unable to be present on the occasion of talking with their child. The reason for this is that the new information about their origins will almost certainly have an impact on the way your child thinks about or reacts to the absent or partially absent parent. If you suspect an ex-partner may 'tell' in a way that is unhelpful for your children if s/he knows you are planning to take this action, then letting your ex know immediately after the 'telling' has taken place will be important for your children.

Some mothers have shared information about sperm donation with their child without letting the father know that this has happened. This is a strategy that comes with the high risk of accidental disclosure, as well as being an unfair burden for a young person to carry. It continues the secret and is likely to unbalance family relationships if parents are still together or in contact. Where children feel resentment towards the parent who is unaware, it is unlikely that they will keep the secret for very long, leading to an unplanned confrontation that benefits no-one.

What is going on for 12 – 16 year olds

Children and young people's development takes place on three main fronts –

- Physical growth that is completed by late teens or early 20s
- Cognitive (thinking and learning) growth, which is at its height in childhood and early teenage years
- Social and emotional growth which continues throughout life

Rates of development in these different areas do not always keep pace with each other – for example a young person may have a growth spurt which leaves them looking older than they are socially and emotionally. Because their brain is undergoing very many changes as it prepares for the move towards adulthood, a young teenager may seem to have gone backwards in their ability to manage their life and emotionally 'tune in' to others. The competencies they had in late childhood can appear to all but vanish as their focus inevitably turns inwards.

Although the rate at which children develop varies enormously, by the time your child is 12 or 13 you are likely to have noticed many changes taking place in their body, mind, emotions and behaviour. Your previously co-operative, enthusiastic and energetic nine or ten year old may have become increasingly private and uncooperative, often retreating from your gaze and your voice to their room or behind screens. There are likely to be many flashes of the child you were familiar with but the increasingly mature conversations and perhaps cuddles last thing at night may well be punctuated with outbursts to rival a toddler's tantrum. The truth is that early adolescence has some similarities to toddlerhood. At both stages there is striving for independence without the emotional maturity to manage it. The difference this time is that your child is (sometimes) as big or bigger than you, is not easily distracted and has the verbal ability to keep answering back. They also no longer idealise you as a parent and so are less eager to please.

Young people often feel at a loss about what is happening to them and parents may feel they are losing the child they knew. Giving up being a child and moving towards adulthood can be a very painful process for children and for parents. Your reactions at this stage may well take you back to your own experiences as a teenager.

A complex combination of changes in the brain, body and hormonal system is taking place during puberty and early adolescence. Although outward physical changes are the most obvious, the most dramatic changes take place unseen in the brain. It is as though the brain were being 're-modelled' in order to be able to work in the more complex ways necessary in adult life. No wonder one of the mostly unspoken questions for young people at this time is, 'Who am I?'

The growing up process has been complicated further since the advent of mobile phones and social media. No longer is home a retreat from the combat of the outside world. Social media follows young people into every nook and cranny of their lives and few are able to resist being constantly present on the latest app or viewing a 'must watch' video.

These are the downsides of both being a teenager and being a parent of one or more as well. There are of course the enormous positives of watching your child grow and change, take baby or giant steps into the grown-up world, develop their talents and begin to emerge towards the fully formed adult they will become.

There is further information about the 12-16 stage in the section on Language and teenage development.

Donor Conception and early adolescence

Starting to share information about donor conception during this stage needs to be done very carefully. Most young people are certainly capable of understanding the facts about their origins at this age. However, emotionally they may be less able to manage and process the information because of the changes, described above, that are taking place. Parents' task is to provide a secure and stable base from which teenagers can test their boundaries. Being told that someone outside the family was involved in their conception can feel like the rug is being pulled out from under their feet. Learning of a third (or fourth person in the case of double or embryo donation) can be quite a shock, as can learning of an egg donor in a child who previously thought they were just sperm donor conceived or in a case of non-gestational surrogacy in a gay male couple. If relationships are already under strain because of teenage behaviour, or anything else that is happening in the family, information about donor conception has the potential to add fuel to the fire.

That said, there are likely to be very good reasons for you wanting or needing to 'tell' at this time so preparing yourself well is the very best thing for you to do.

Teenagers have one foot in childhood and another striving towards adulthood (and the proportion of each will differ according to both how old they are and how mature their psychological development is). When you are 'telling' it is helpful to appeal to their more adult side. You can do this by saying you feel they are old enough now to have this information, which will belong to them and is their right to have, although you will always be there to answer questions and support them in their feelings and in any actions they need to take. Even with 12 year olds and younger teenagers it is always right, unless your child has learning difficulties, to use direct language and terminology, explaining afterwards if necessary. Some young teenagers are fascinated by the science of IVF, but don't let long conversations about the details of your treatment get in the way of talking about feelings.

Telling

You may want to think up and rehearse a 'script' for the occasion of telling or you may be more comfortable allowing the words to flow naturally on the day. Alternatively, you may feel you could best express yourself by first writing a letter that your child could read in your presence. Whichever way you choose to do it, remember that you are starting to tell a story that will be on-going.

If you are part of a couple it may be that both of you will be involved in telling your child or it may just be one of you for some reason. Whether the telling is done by one or both parents these guidelines have been put together following many discussions with donor-conceived young people and their parents. Here are some of things to consider before going ahead with telling -

Children first – put the emotional needs of your child first but remember this is not a time for babying. They will appreciate direct language. This is the story of how they made you a family. The story of your infertility can come later. Share information with all your children (including those who came into the family other than by donor conception) either at the same time or within a very short space of time. If you have much younger donor conceived children as well, you may want to start 'telling' them in a way that is appropriate for their age on a different day (see the booklet focused on their age group).

Stage of development – Bearing in mind that young teenage years can be a time of emotional turmoil, try to choose a time when relationships in the family are good or as good as they are likely to be. If you have the option, you may choose to postpone 'telling' until the emotional climate feels more settled.

Preparation – think through what you want to say and why, including a clear but short explanation about why you have chosen to tell them now and not before. Don't be shy about talking it through with a trusted friend, a family member or professional counsellor – it may well help you feel more confident.

Support – make sure there is someone in place that you can take your feelings to afterwards. Don't burden your child with any strong and/or difficult feelings you may have.

Your child may or may not need some outside support as well so have in mind some suggestions for people they could talk to or let them know about on-line resources (see Links at the end of the booklet).

Timing – choose a time when there are no other significant events going on in your child's life, such as exams or relationship issues, and make sure you have sufficient time after telling for any immediate response, questions and discussion. Don't make an appointment to 'tell them something important'. They are likely to worry themselves sick that you are going to tell them you have a cancer diagnosis or, if you are a couple, that you are about to divorce. Try instead to use a time when you would naturally be together.

Place – home is better than a public place or a holiday resort. Your child may well need to be able to retreat to a familiar space of their own and/or contact a friend. If it feels natural and appropriate consider doing the 'telling' whilst you are out walking, doing some cooking or having a meal with your child. It is sometimes easier to talk side by side rather than face to face. Walking in a park or countryside is going to be better than a busy street. A car ride together can be a good place for continuing conversations but probably not right for first time 'telling'.

Language – be direct in the way you explain about how they came to be part of the family. Give information clearly and simply and don't get so hung up on technicalities that you forget to speak with warmth about how much they were wanted and how loved they are. Too much detail about why you couldn't conceive is unnecessary. This age-group is particularly embarrassed by the idea that their parents might have had sex at all! The following is an example of how such a conversation could be started. It can be adapted as necessary for other situations. –

> "Dad and I have something we want to talk to you about. Don't worry, we are both well and not thinking of getting a divorce, but it is something important about you and how we became a family. Dad and I always wanted to become parents but it wasn't happening for us. When we consulted a doctor we discovered that my eggs had run out/weren't working well and so with the help of a clinic/hospital we used an egg from another woman, a donor, to help make you. We couldn't believe our luck when I became pregnant and when you were born we were over the moon. We loved you then and haven't stopped loving you since. I imagine this is a bit of a shock but we felt you had the right to know."

One thing at a time – give the basic information first and resist the temptation to heap more on them until they are ready. News like this takes time to sink in.

Acknowledge how your child may be feeling and show that you understand, without becoming defensive. Sentences beginning in the following ways can be helpful –

I imagine that…*(this is pretty difficult for you to take in etc.)*
You may be feeling… *(confused, upset or angry that we have not told you before etc.)*
It would be very understandable…*(if you had a lot of mixed feelings going round inside you about this etc.)*

Although these are useful phrases to use it is also helpful to recognise that just because we have a certain feeling about something, another person may not feel the same way. You and your child will each have your own unique perceptions.

This action of 'telling' isn't a one-off or linear process either. Your child might very quickly jump to related topics before you think they have taken in the basic facts – asking what you know about their donor, how they can look for him/her/them, and whether they have half-siblings from the same donor. It's all part of working through the implications of what you are telling them.

Follow up – let your child know that this is a safe subject to talk about and that you are willing to discuss anything at a mutually convenient time. It is a good idea to initiate a conversation within a couple of weeks or so (and in the future) just to check how they are feeling and let them know that you are happy to talk at any time.

Margaret told her 18 year old daughter and 13 year old son of their dc origins, and explained afterwards in an article in the DCN Journal, "I have asked her how she feels since being told and she said she feels fine, but also finds it strange that there is someone out there who helped make her that she will never know, and how she won't know about her whole medical history etc but that she also doesn't know if she would want to meet him even if she could...so I think she's dealing with a few different emotions but pretty much seems her usual self at the moment...I feel so relieved that they now know, although I do feel a sense of upset for them...I have told them both to come and talk to me about anything at any time, no matter what emotions they are feeling as I want to be there for them."

You may have quite complicated feelings about other people knowing how your child was conceived but please don't ask your child to keep the news quiet. Continuing the secret is an unfair burden for your child to take on. It is now their information to pass on to others or not, as they see fit. It is probably a good idea to mention to your child that using social media to share this information with friends is potentially something they may regret in the future, so best to talk over the phone or private messaging with individual chosen friends whilst the information is new. You may also want to discuss who should be told in the extended family and who will undertake to do this. If your child is still 12, 13 or 14 you may want to suggest doing the 'telling' in tandem but don't be surprised if they prefer the privacy to choose who should know and how this should happen. Privacy is what everyone is entitled to whilst secrecy with its overtones of shame is to be avoided.

Telling about a second donor or the use of egg donation in surrogacy

Many single women who have used double or embryo donation to have their children, will by this age have told them about the sperm donor. However, it is sometimes not until children are approaching their teens that they reveal that there was an egg donor as well.

If this is your situation, you may have quite a complicated mixture of feelings about why it has felt so difficult to include the egg donor in conversations with your child about donor conception. It is sometimes only after many years of parenting and feeling secure in the relationship with a child that solo mums feel that the time has come to 'tell' about the egg donor as well.

As part of your preparation for adding in this information it can be helpful to think about your particular reasons for not having shared this before. Are there are any left-over issues you need to resolve yourself before talking with your child? Other single women with experience of talking with an older child about egg donation are likely to be happy to support you – many DC Network members have grappled with this situation.

When it comes to the actual 'telling' it is helpful to both you and your children to be as confident as possible and perhaps link the information to questions that have arisen in the past or recently about looks, talents or interests. As part of your child's story has already been shared, this can be a useful 'hook' to hang the further information on. All the previous guidance about 'telling' for the first time is of course relevant as well in this situation.

Where **surrogacy** has been used as part of assisted reproduction it is sometimes quite easy for couples (gay, lesbian or heterosexual) to forget that an egg donor (the surrogate herself or a separate donor) has been part of the creation of a child because the emphasis is on the third party gestation. It may not be until the child is approaching teenage years and possibly questioning looks, traits and talents that it becomes clear that information about the egg donor should be included as part of their story. Again it is a good idea for couples to think about their particular reasons for not having shared this information before and if there are any left-over feelings that need to be resolved before 'telling'. The guidance given to solo mums above and all the general guidance about 'telling' is relevant for this situation also.

Heterosexual couples who have used double or embryo donation may also have been putting off the moment of revealing their fully non-genetic relationship to their child or children. There may be even greater anxiety about rejection because of the double donation. If this is your situation then good preparation along the lines suggested above will be necessary, together with talking with your child about positively choosing to become a parent and the loving care and nurture that has happened as part of carrying them during pregnancy.

Reactions to Being 'Told'

Will my child reject me?

The fear of rejection is huge for many mums and dads but the experience of the vast majority of parents that DC Network knows of, is that this has not happened. However, you need to be prepared for a whole range of positive, negative, ambivalent and indifferent feelings. Some teenagers react with anger and hurt at being told something they don't understand properly, that they feel has been kept from them and that complicates further their struggles to navigate towards a new image of the sort of person they want to be in adult life.

As has been discussed earlier, your child is at an important transition in their life. Not quite a child any more but certainly not an adult yet. Their response to the news you are planning to give them is likely to be influenced by the circumstances under which they have been told, your readiness to accept their initial reaction, whatever it is, and your willingness to talk about the subject when they need to do so. This being an unpredictable age, the immediate reaction of each child may vary from almost no outward sign at all to unconcealed shock, disbelief and anger. At the time there may be many questions or none at all. A calm response may or may not hide a turbulence of feelings underneath, but one way or another there is likely to be a lot going on in their heads over the following few days, weeks and months.

Emma, who learned about her donor conception a few months before her 14th birthday, reflects 10 years on about how she felt immediately after being told –

"Shell shocked I think is the only way to describe it! I wanted to find out everything I could from my mum and bombarded her with questions. It wasn't until I was on my own that I remember having all these different feelings rushing about. It felt so strange to realise that I have no biological connection to my dad's side of the family, my nana and granpy, aunts, uncles and cousins. I can remember thinking 'so where does my artistic side come from then?' now that I couldn't relate it to my uncle (who's an artist). I was also intrigued about the donor and started wondering about him, how much I was like him, whether I looked like him and what he would be like."

In 2018 Frances, who is divorced from her husband, told her nearly 13 year old twins Ben and Polly about being conceived via egg donation. She wrote to tell me how it went –

"I actually sat down with Ben and Polly yesterday and went ahead with the conversation…predictably it was harrowing…all the emotions were there, sadness, anger, disbelief…but after a few hours which were very difficult, they were already starting to come to their own conclusions that in fact the news changes nothing. My daughter is the most vocal about it and wants to ask questions all the time. My son is less vocal and claims he's fine with it as "I'm his mum"…whatever…but I think once he's pondered it more he may have a different reaction. The overarching feeling from Polly was one of disappointment that we don't share the same DNA (she loves watching crime programmes) but we discussed at length what we do share. She has also indicated that she would like to talk to someone else in a similar position and I've said I will investigate that for her. So probably one of the most difficult conversations I've ever had…but it's ongoing and they're puttering around today doing the usual things. Thanks again for all your help"

The power of secrets

It may not just be the information itself that will have an impact, but also the fact that a secret has been kept. The older your child is the more likely they are to question why they have not been told before. Adults who are told for the first time often describe feeling shocked to the point of being knocked off balance by the information. Under 16s may experience similar feelings as well as anger, sadness or occasionally relief if the news is felt to answer questions of dissimilarity between family members or gaps in information that have puzzled them over the years.

A donor conceived adult in the USA has spoken about the deception involved in keeping such an important secret being much more hurtful than the fact of donor conception itself. On disclosure this is sometimes experienced as parents having power over their children. If a lot of other people have known whilst your child has not, then this too may be upsetting for them.

There may also be a questioning of trust – "Can I believe you in the future?" and 'What else haven't you told me?" are typical questions that represent the loss of a previously unquestioned relationship.

Who am I?

This is the mostly unspoken question that is the driving force behind much of the often testing and experimental behaviour of young teenagers. Their task is to emerge from the chrysalis of the person who, up until this point in their life, has been largely shaped by the conditions of their upbringing. New information about their biological background throws another element into this quest for identity – "What have the genes I have inherited from my donor given me?" As young people are often preoccupied by their rapidly changing appearance, it may well be physical likeness that becomes the focus of their questioning around identity.

The issue of physical or other likeness may well have already come up in your family, particularly if your child does not look anything like any other family member. Some donor conceived children and adults who do not fit in with the physical, intellectual or creative characteristics in a family have asked if they have been adopted or wondered privately if they were the result of their mother having an affair.

Physical likeness seems to be important because it is seen as connecting families together over time. As human beings we establish who we are at least partly in relation to who we think our parents and family are. This new knowledge about half or all of their genetic inheritance means that your child is likely to need some time to re-appraise themselves, your family and their relationships. Adjustment to the new situation may come quickly or take quite a while, depending on their individual personality and temperament, how they are managing teenage years generally and other things that may be going on in your or their lives.

Donor conception throws up difficult questions for parents and for children about the importance of genetics. And there are no straightforward answers. If you have always found it easier to cope with the idea of your donor by visualising, say a donor egg, as 'just a clump of cells', then it's not easy to begin to think of her as a living human being. But it is possible that your child will want to find someone who looks like them, or shares their talents and passions. If you believe that nurture is what influences a child's upbringing most, then it may take further thought to reconcile this with the immense fascination of genealogy as a hobby, as demonstrated in the long-running TV show 'Who Do You Think You Are' and the runaway success of direct-to-consumer DNA testing companies.

It may take some time for initial and subsequent feelings to be worked through, but if you can keep the lines of communication open, then at some point – possibly not until years later – your more mature young adult may be able to understand and appreciate the difficulties that you as parent(s) have been through.

Siblings in your family

If your child has grown up with brothers and sisters, then some of the first questions are likely to be about their relatedness to them. If you have other children by donor conception they may or may not share the same donor. You may also have adopted children or have a child conceived without reproductive assistance. The revelation that brothers and sisters may not be fully biologically related can be a very powerful one to have to cope with. Responses are likely to vary depending on the meaning of the information for the siblings involved, but it can initially be felt as devastating.

There are both advantages and disadvantages to a situation where siblings have been conceived by different donors. If, for instance, one sibling wishes to search for their donor or half-siblings and the other does not, then it may be an advantage if they do not share a donor. But where both siblings wish to have information, it may be more difficult if one is able to make a connection and the other is not. When siblings do share a donor it is important that differing needs for information are taken into account and respected, although this may be tricky to manage practically.

Where there are siblings conceived without reproductive assistance it will be particularly important to give reassurance that the donor conceived person is loved equally. Following 'telling' children are likely to think back to how their parents have behaved towards each sibling in the past.

Half-siblings

In addition to any children the donor has, there may well be half-siblings in the families of other people who have used the same donor. In the case of sperm donation there could be children in a total of 10 families (including yours) if you conceived in the UK. If you conceived abroad or in the UK with sperm imported from an overseas clinic or bank, there could be very many more around the world. The existence of half-siblings was something not often contemplated by people receiving donated eggs or sperm at the time you had your treatment so you may have difficulty getting your head round this. Imagine how mind blowing the existence of many half-siblings might be to a teenager who has just learned of their origins. Thoughts about these latter half-siblings may not come immediately but only on realisation that their donor did not exclusively donate for their parent(s). Once the possibility of many half-siblings is recognised there may be more interest in them than their donor. Damian, who was told about his origins when he was young, is typical of many donor conceived young people in being more interested in his half-siblings than his donor –

> "I'd be more interested in finding out about any brothers and sisters. This is because we'd be the same sort of age, they might be like me, they might be interested in the same sort of stuff as me. I would definitely be interested in meeting them."

The donor

It is likely that at some point in the re-appraisal process your child will ask questions about their donor and it would be a mistake to assume that a happy, well balanced child 'shouldn't be' interested in their donor.

The sort of information they are looking for can include both non-identifying information such as medical history, physical characteristics and ethnic and cultural background, as well as more personal information about the donor's interests and values. This desire for information is very natural and part of the process of making sense of the new information and the implications for their identity. They may also be interested in the donor's family, particularly if they have had any children as they would be half-siblings to them.

> Natasha, sperm donor conceived and now in her twenties, pointed out in a talk to a DC Network conference, that it is perfectly possible to be a happy and fulfilled person AND be very curious about her donor.

Searching for genetic connections

At this stage your child may or may not want to search for information about their donor or half-siblings. If they do want more information than you are able to give them, being able to access it will depend partly on where they were conceived and also the date of their conception. If they were conceived in the UK on or after April 2005 your child will be entitled to identifying information from age 18. This is true whether the sperm or eggs originated in the UK or were imported from abroad. It is important to remember however, that no matter what the donor signed up to a number of years previously, they may in fact be difficult or impossible to trace, have changed their mind about accepting the responsibility of contact, or be seriously ill or have died.

At 18 donor conceived adults conceived at any time after August 1991 can also register with the HFEA (Human Fertilisation and Embryology Authority) to be in touch with half-siblings by mutual consent.

If you conceived before April 2005 then the donor will remain anonymous, except in cases where the man or woman has re-registered with the HFEA as being willing to become identifiable. It has been possible for donors to do this since 2005. At age 16 both pre and post 2005 conception children can apply to the HFEA to find out if they are donor conceived, ask for any further non-identifying details that the HFEA may hold (sometimes they have more than clinics have revealed to parents) and also ask for the number, years of birth and gender of any half-siblings. Prior to age 16 parents may ask for this information on behalf of their children.

If your child was conceived abroad then you and your child will be entitled to information according to the laws of that country. Contrary to the expectations and assumptions of some parents, being introduced to your overseas clinic by a UK doctor does not mean that a record of your treatment and your child's details will appear on the HFEA register and entitle them to the information above.

Another way to trace genetic relatives has become possible only very recently. Direct to Consumer DNA testing where a simple kit is obtained from a company and saliva (spit) is obtained in a tube and returned for testing, has become very popular in the US, Scandinavia and the UK and is rapidly spreading round the world. Most people use it in addition to paper research about family history but increasingly unexpected results are revealing unknown relatives and family secrets that sometimes involve donor conception. Donor conceived people are using the tests to discover genetic relatives and many are finding donors and half-siblings. This can bring great joy, peace of mind and a sense of validation to their identity. It is a risky business, however, as some people have felt sorrow and confusion when donors who had expected to remain anonymous, refuse contact, or half-siblings turn out to be people with whom your child has nothing in common.

If your child is interested in doing a DNA test it is a good idea to think through the pros and cons first and if you decide to go ahead, possibly treat it as a family project with you all sending in saliva samples. In the case of sperm donation it is helpful for the mother to also be tested in order to rule out her DNA in the child's results and for dad to be tested in the case of egg donation. It's also worth considering the terms on which you sign up to these companies as your DNA may become their property.

How you feel about all this is another question! You may well have ambivalent or, even more strongly, fearful feelings about your child searching for their donor or half-siblings. However, evidence from stories told by donor conceived adults and young people shows that parents who are able to accept that this is a very normal response and who remain calm, confident and supportive, are likely to be rewarded in the long term with a stronger relationship, even if things are a little uncertain for a while. It has also become clear that parents being fearful, uninterested or unwilling to engage with their children in their interest in genetic connections, does not stop them from searching. They will just do it anyway behind your back.

It is much better for family relations if you can deal with your feelings elsewhere and be as supportive as you can when talking with your children about their needs and wishes.

Some parents feel that they themselves should search for as much information as they can before they talk with their children. As strong as this impulse may be it is almost certainly better resisted as such actions could be interpreted as 'taking over' or exerting power over information that rightly belongs to your child. It may be better instead to let your child know that you are willing to help and support them in any way you can if they decide they want to try and obtain more information.

Some donor conceived people feel a great need to find out as much information as possible whilst others have a less urgent curiosity and still others do not feel the need to search at all. In this they are very similar to adopted people. Some 12 to 16 year olds may well be curious about their donor but choose not to search or even ask many questions. This may be because they are pre-occupied with growing up or other things going on in their lives, but it may also indicate a perceived need to protect parents from their quite difficult feelings. They love you very much and need you not to be upset by how they feel or what they want to do. Other young people may be openly engaged by donor conception issues from the moment of being 'told'. For those for whom more information feels important, finding that their access is blocked by the law or 'the system' as some refer to it, (in the UK or abroad) may trigger strong feelings. If your child wants to start searching soon after being 'told' you may want to encourage them to wait a while in order for first feelings to settle down. But beyond recommending caution, your support for whatever they decide they need to do is likely to be valued.

An Australian donor conceived adult who was 'told' about her beginnings at age 15, reflects seven years on that it can take some time for interest in genetic history to develop –

Investigating the links at the end of this leaflet could be a shared project, but leave it to your child to instigate the search once they have the information.

Talking

Language and teenage development

Throughout this booklet the term 'donor' has been used to refer to the man or woman who gave their sperm or eggs to help build your family and you are likely to employ this word during the 'telling' process. A parent using the word 'father' or 'mother' by itself or 'real father or mother' to refer to the donor can confuse the role of the person who gave their gametes with that of the person who has loved and actively fathered or mothered a child from birth. But the donor has an undeniable genetic connection to the children he or she helped to create and your child may want to use a term other than 'donor' to refer to him or her.

As your child or children grapple with the new information you have given them about themselves their language when referring to the probably unknown man and/or woman who helped to make them, may change from day to day and not settle down for several months, or even years. Young people, making rational and conventional links between genes and inheritance, may use the term 'real mother or father' but without any intention to disturb or harm the emotional relationship s/he has with their non-genetic parent. Teenagers are experimenting with the world and their place in it, so it is not surprising that they might try out different words to describe the man or woman who helped to make them and their relationship to this person. Biological mother or father is common or perhaps shortened to 'bio mum or dad' as they become more comfortable with the concept of having someone outside their immediate family with whom they share something fundamental but do not have a social or emotional relationship with, (unless their donor is a family member or friend). As likely as not, the terms they choose to use will vary even within the same sentence as they play with language and the meaning of being donor conceived.

By 17 or so the words young people use are likely to settle down along with the more complex thinking capacity that has developed by this age. Older teenagers have largely moved on from the very 'me' focussed early teen years to be able to see the world from more than one perspective. They are more able to 'tune-in' to the feelings of others and significant interest and curiosity about their donor and half-siblings can co-exist with an acknowledgement of their non-genetic parent as their 'real' father or mother. They may even be able to show empathy to you about the difficult times you have been through and the hard decisions you had to make.

In most solo parent and lesbian/gay households, where only one donor has been used, children will have had their origins explained to them long before the age of 12. Twelve to sixteen year olds in lone parent households will not have issues with language in quite the same way as there is no father/mother in the house to confuse with the donor. In lesbian households there is a genetic and non-genetic connection that may have been acknowledged over the years by the terminology used, eg. Mum and Mama. This may or may not feel more complicated if one partner has donated eggs to the other, but there will always remain a male person who helped to create your child and who may or may not be part of your life. The same recognition of genetic and non-genetic parents may also be acknowledged by the naming of each parent in male couple households

Robyn is 21, her feelings and the language she uses about her egg donor Angie, may or may not be mirrored by your child if they choose to look for their donor.

It's a big sense of relief to have Angie in my life, and nice to have the missing half of my identity confirmed... It's like the relationship you'd have with an aunt, it's really nice. We're both navigating this very weird situation together. We address each other by our names – if I'm talking about her to someone else, she's my 'egg donor'. I respect my mum so much, I wouldn't call Angie my 'biological mum' or use any variation of the word 'mum'. But a lot of people, especially people whose mums are still alive, call their donor their 'biological mother' or 'biological father'.

How parents feel about language issues

You may have it very clear in your head that the donor was just that, an anonymous someone who provided the missing ingredient when you or you and your partner desperately wanted to become parent(s). But no matter how much you use the term 'donor' your child may have other ideas and may make these explicit by his or her use of different terminology, which, as discussed above, may change over time. This can feel very uncomfortable. Your first instinct may be to react defensively but it is helpful to try and remember that they are in the process of working things out for themselves and that any strong response from you is likely to be counter-productive.

Twelve to 16 year olds are practising independence very hard and will sometimes say things simply to wind parents up or in the words of the mother of a 14 year old boy, "put clear blue water" between his views and hers. Whether it is used as a challenge to your authority or because of strongly felt emotions, it is always good to recall that a lot of processing is going on and that it's all part of your child getting to grips with what donor conception really means for them at the same time as learning to think for themselves.

It can also be helpful to remind yourself that 12 – 16 is a very uncomfortable age in children's lives. They will often find themselves behaving in ways that feel out of their control and look to parents to provide security and clear but reasonable limits so that they can feel safe. Of course at the time it may feel to you like yet another argument instead of a cry for help, but a clear, firm and friendly response can often help teenagers begin to develop ways of taking charge of their own feelings and behaviour.

Talking with others

School matters

Modern secondary education offers many opportunities for debate on moral and ethical issues. Sex and relationship education may or may not include anything about the different ways families are made, while biology lessons concentrate on facts rather than feelings. These sessions have the potential to stir up feelings to do with donor conception and may be particularly difficult for young people who have only recently learned of their origins.

Some children who have known from early on about their beginnings by donor conception are happy to have their say in lessons referring to family formation or biological creation. However, most children who have only just learned that their origins are different to those they had previously believed, are unlikely to speak up and may feel quite intimidated by lesson content that comes close to the difficult or mixed feelings they are juggling. They will also be very aware of the potential for the information to get on to social media where responses cannot be guaranteed to be informed or supportive.

It can be helpful for parents to find out what the school curriculum contains at this stage, watch out for any difficulties a child may be having and consider whether or not they are related to the processing of new information about being DC. In addition to offering your child support and discussion at home you may want to talk with your child about whether it would be worthwhile to (selectively and privately) share some information with an appropriate teacher.

Katherine, who is in a lesbian partnership and the mother of Milly, wrote to the Network about how a discussion has been prompted in her household by a debate held at her daughter's school –

> "It has also been another significant time for Milly and us around 'telling' and feelings raised about being donor conceived. This was triggered by an ethical debate in GCSE religion around methods of conception and becoming parents and 'multiple parentage' – gamete donation, surrogacy and legal parents. All quite heavy material for a 14 year old, especially one who has chosen to be so private about her donor conception as a teenager."

Telling others

A newly 'told' teenager is unlikely to want to share this new information with anyone other than his or her most trusted friends, not least because of the likelihood of it being spread around on social media. Not that being donor conceived is anything to be ashamed of but whilst a young person is grappling with what it means for them, it is unhelpful to find everyone else knows and has their own opinion about it. It may be that your child is reluctant to tell anyone else because of the danger of social media exposure, but this could leave them without an outlet for their thoughts and feelings. Talk with your child about this and explore together who might be a good person to share information with. It may be that they have a close relationship with a god-parent or extended family member or friend who could be trusted to listen and not spread information around. DC Network can sometimes offer support in the form of a slightly older DC person to talk to. There is also a Facebook group specifically for young donor conceived people to be able to share information and gain support (see information at end of booklet).

As a young person growing towards independence your child will be in charge of the information of who else should know, but you may want to discuss with them handling situations such as seeing a doctor for the first time since finding out about being donor conceived. If your child is still young and you are accompanying them to see a doctor you need to decide jointly beforehand who will explain about DC when/if the doctor asks about family history. Other contacts with the medical profession may not require the sharing of this essentially private information and offer opportunities for young people to decide for themselves whether they wish to 'tell' or not.

Helen, mother to two teenage sons, says, "It's like a see-saw; it's not a 'handing over' moment of 'right, it's your information now and you decide what you're going to do with it.' It's more that sometimes your teenager might feel they want to be entirely in charge, whilst at other times they might want the choice of asking you to deal with telling the GP or whoever it is."

Jane realised just how mature her 16 year old son Simon, conceived through sperm donation, had become when a sports injury took them to the local Accident and Emergency department. A nurse commented on Simon's 6ft 4in height and asked if he took after his father. Resisting her first urge to jump in and take over Jane decided to let Simon speak for himself. Simon commented that he "Didn't take after his dad but his grandad was tall." The nurse then said, "Well I wonder who you do take after then?" and looking at Jane, with eyes sparkling with humour, Simon responded, "Goodness knows." Jane felt so proud of her son as he had decided for himself how he would deal with that moment. He knew exactly what he was saying and why he was saying it.

Single Parents and Same Sex Families

Children of single people and gay or lesbian parents will already be dealing with the way in which their families are different from those where there is a father/mother present or living separately. In early teenage years they may need to distance themselves from this reality as they struggle to be as much like their peers as possible. Solo mums and lesbian families are already likely to have told their children that a man (known or unknown) gave his sperm so that they could be conceived. Children in solo dad or gay families will know that a surrogate (known or unknown) carried them for their parent(s). However, they may not be aware that another woman may have been involved in their conception: an egg donor. This would also be the case for children conceived by double or embryo donation. Ideally a child will know about all the people involved in their conception from an early age but sometimes a donor, usually the woman who gave her egg, is missed out. The section on Telling (p9) gives guidance if this is your situation.

The teenage years for those children with gay, lesbian or solo mum parents may already be feeling quite difficult because of the obvious 'difference' in their family to those of their peers, although this generation of teenagers is much more used to diversity in family type than previous ones. Feelings of 'difference' will vary individually and may also be influenced by where the family is living, urban metropolises being easier than small towns or country villages. Being donor conceived may or may not feel like an additional burden for a while and this is another reason for finding a time when things feel settled in the family to share anything your teenager does not already know.

If things are feeling a bit frazzled in your family at this time you may want to console yourself with knowing that most families go through difficult times during teenage years, with children feeling embarrassed about their parents and wanting to distance themselves from them for a range of spurious reasons. Do your best to keep the lines of communication open and things are likely to change as they get older.

Final Thoughts

Making the decision that your child should have the information about how they came into your family, or additional information relating to double donation or surrogacy, may have taken you beyond where you would normally feel comfortable emotionally. None of us likes to be in this place for very long. It is impossible to say how your child or children will take the news but it is very rare for a donor conceived young person to say that they would have preferred not to know.

This booklet has focused a lot on the developmental stage of your child. This is because it is often not an easy one for either parent(s) or children. Sharing information about donor conception may rock the boat for a while but most families are resilient and many of you reading this will have been through challenging times before and bounced back. Acknowledgement of donor conception can sometimes shed light on family relationships that have felt blocked, freeing members to recognise and accept differences that felt risky whilst the secret was being kept. It creates the possibility for improved communication and greater family closeness, but this may be only after a period of uncertainty. Your child or children will need to know that they are much loved, despite any behaviour that on the surface may not seem very lovable. It can be helpful to take every genuine opportunity to praise and support them, but this does not mean becoming a pushover because you are worried about how they are feeling, or feeling guilty yourself for not 'telling' them earlier. Remaining in charge and using your parental authority sparingly and wisely is exactly what they need to feel loved and secure.

The final words are from two mothers of children who were 'told' between the ages of 12 and 16. The first, chose with her partner, to create their family by anonymous sperm donation because of male infertility.

She had had a very difficult relationship with her daughter, but now reflects from five years on about the change that came over time following telling her daughter the truth about donor conception –

"I had lied to her for the first 16 years of her life and I blamed that wall (one we couldn't talk through) for our difficulty with communication. As we have progressed together through this maze and learned to trust each other, the flood of communication is amazing. She and I can now understand and explore each other's thoughts with clarity. Granted, she has matured and now allows concepts to be discussed that previously were 'not her thing', but I see the difference in our relationship based on truth-telling, more than her maturing over time."

Frances, whose email to me following 'telling' her nearly 13 year old egg donation twins, was quoted earlier, contacted me again recently. She is divorced from Ben and Polly's genetic father who has chosen not to have further contact with them and declined to take part in the occasion of 'telling'.

"At this point I feel very lucky that my lovely brave twins have taken it so well.... although I'm under no illusion that this will stay as such.... as they go through their teenage years I'm sure there may well be occasions when one or both of them might throw the ' you're not my real mother' card at me at a time of angst. I worry a little about my son who was so calm about it all and even when I mentioned it a few weeks ago he just said...' it's all fine.... I don't see you as anything but my mum'.
One thing I'm really glad I did before 'telling' was to fulfil a promise I had made to Ben and Polly to buy a dog once they were 12. I didn't do this as 'compensation for the news to come' but because I knew from colleagues at work and another friend, that pets as therapy at times of stress, can be a great comfort and grounder. I do believe that Biscuit played a huge role in comforting and distracting both the children at the time of 'telling' them.

Further Reading

Most of the social and emotional issues around donor conception have remained the same for many years, despite the fertility, social media and technology worlds having changed significantly in many other ways. The books below remain as relevant today as when they were written and their knowledge and wisdom will help you further explore both the current and lifetime issues associated with sharing information about donor conception with your child.

- Ken Daniels.
  Building a family with the assistance of donor insemination
  (Dunmore Press, Palmerston North, 2004)
  Available to buy in the UK only from
  DC Network

- Diane Ehrensaft.
  Mommies, daddies, donors, surrogates: answering tough questions and building strong families
  (The Guilford Press, New York London, 2005)

- Ellen Sarasohn Glazer and Evelina Weidman Sterling.
  Having your baby through egg donation
  (Second edition, Jessica Kingsley Publishers, London, 2013)

- Wendy Kramer and Naomi Cahn, J.D.
  Finding our families: A first-of-its-kind book for donor conceived people and their families
  (Penguin group, New York, 2013)

- Olivia Montuschi.
  'You're not my father anyway…'
  March 2005, in Personal Stories on the Donor Conception Network website:
  www.dcnetwork.org

- Jana Rupnow
  Three makes Baby: How to parent your donor conceived child
  2018 Rupnow Associates publishing
  Available to buy from DC Network website

For those who like ideas and research studies

- Petra Nordqvist and Carol Smart.
  Relative Strangers: Family life, genes and donor conception
  (Palgrave MacMillan Hampshire, 2014)

- Katherine Fine (editor).
  Donor Conception for Life: Psychoanalytic Reflections on New Ways of Conceiving the Family
  (Karnac London, 2015)
  Available to buy from DC Network

- Susan Golombok.
  Modern Families: Parents and Children in New Family Forms
  (Cambridge University Press, Cambridge, 2015)

Parenting and child development

- Nicola Morgan.
  Blame my brain: the amazing teenage brain revealed
  (Walker Books, London, 2005)

- Daniel J. Siegel, MD
  Brainstorm: The Purpose and Power of the Teenage Brain
  Scribe UK 2017

- Josh Shipp
  The Grown-Ups Guide to Teenage Humans
  Harper Wave 2017

- Adele Faber and Elaine Mazlish
  How to Talk So Teens Will Listen and Listen So Teens Will Talk
  Templar Publishing 2006

Continued…

Further Reading

For Young Teenagers

* Beverley Ward
  Archie Nolan: Family Detective,
  Donor Conception Network, UK, 2015

  A humorous, illustrated story book along the
  lines of the Diary of a Wimpy Kid books
  featuring Archie and his twin sister Jemima
  who are donor conceived.

* Annabelle Pitcher
  Silence is Goldfish
  UK, 2005

  15 year old Tess discovers by accident that
  she is donor conceived. Her subsequent
  refusal/inability to speak masks the turbulence
  of feelings and questions she is grappling
  with. A torch in the shape of a goldfish aids
  her quest for the truth.

Social Media

There are many Facebook groups for donor
conceived adults but the only one that is
appropriate for 12 to 16 year olds is –
Generation Z Donor Conceived People. Here
young people can talk with each other about
their thoughts and feelings on being donor
conceived. These groups are either 'secret'
or 'private,' two Facebook categories for
groups, and as such are safe spaces for
young people to open up and get support.

Useful Contacts

British Infertility Counselling Association (BICA)
Website, including Find a Counsellor facility: www.bica.net
info@bica.net

Donor Sibling Registry (DSR)
https://www.donorsiblingregistry.com/

The largest and most comprehensive site for connecting donor offspring/ donors/half-siblings. Started in the US by Wendy Kramer and her sperm donor conceived son Ryan, it has many entries for UK clinics. In addition to the registry there is an excellent section giving access to up to date research and many ways of connecting with and exploring donor conception issues with others.

Human Fertilisation and Embryology Authority
10 Spring Gardens
London SW1A 2BU
Tel: 020 7291 8200
Website: hfea.gov.uk
Email: enquiriesteam.hfea.gov.uk or openingtheregister@hfea.gov.uk